Time Management

Acquire Time Management Abilities And Suggestions For Organizing Your Life, Increasing Productivity, Saving Time, And Achieving Your Objectives Immediately

(Effective To-do List Strategies For Enhancing Productivity And Achieving Task Completion)

Antoine Jackson

TABLE OF CONTENT

Overcoming Obstacles And Maintaining Motivation 1

Concluding Remarks: Specializing In Time Management 6

Procedure For Putting The Selected Strategy Into Action 26

Practicing Mindfulness And Managing One's Thoughts 45

Is It Urgent Or Just Important? 69

Acquiring Knowledge From Errors 94

Timestamp Management For Hardwareren And Parents 127

Overcoming Obstacles And Maintaining Motivation

Typical Time Management Difficulties

Running into obstacles during the time management procedure that could reduce our effectiveness and production is typical.

We'll review some typical problems and solutions in this chapter.

Controlling Your Procrastination

One of the biggest challenges to time management is procrastination.

The following strategies will assist you in overcoming procrastination:

Split Up the Work: Divide more complex jobs into smaller, more doable steps.

This lessens the sense of overwhelm and facilitates getting started.

Establish Reasonable Deadlines: Give your assignments reasonable due dates and commit to meeting them.

This fosters motivation and a sense of urgency.

Apply Productivity Strategies: To boost productivity and combat procrastination, try methods like the Pomodoro Technique, which involves working in concentrated blocks of time (for instance, 25 minutes of intense work followed by a 5-minute break).

Setting Boundaries and Making Self-Care a Priority

A healthy work-life balance requires setting boundaries and giving self-care priority. Lack of limits puts a person at risk for stress and overwhelm, which can result in burnout and other mental health problems. It is crucial to understand that business and personal life shouldn't mix and that a healthy distance between the two is maintained by defining limits.

Setting self-care as a top priority is crucial because it allows people to revitalize and recharge, improving their productivity and efficiency in their personal and professional lives. Reducing stress and preserving physical and mental health need self-care practices, including exercising, getting enough sleep, practising mindfulness, and taking up hobbies.

As a result, creating boundaries and placing self-care first is essential to attaining a positive work-life balance, promoting better general well-being.

Promoting Recreational Activities and Healthy Relationships

A healthy work-life balance requires cultivating wholesome connections and participating in leisure activities. Positive relationships with coworkers, friends, and family lowers stress, offers support, and boosts happiness. To avoid burnout and preserve a healthy work-life balance, scheduling time for interacting with people and forming relationships outside of work is crucial.

Leisure time activities are just as vital since they give people a way to release tension and enhance their sense of well-being. After a demanding workday, hobbies like reading, drawing, dancing, or sports can be a great way to unwind and rejuvenate. To keep work and personal life in harmony, making time for these activities regularly is imperative.

Participating in recreational activities can also increase the effectiveness and productivity of work. Engaging in recreational activities during work breaks has lowered stress, boosted creativity, and enhanced focus and concentration.

In conclusion, maintaining wholesome connections and finding leisure time are critical components of a successful work-life balance. People can lower stress, enhance general well-being, and become more productive and efficient in both their personal and professional lives by scheduling time for these activities.

Concluding Remarks: Specializing In Time Management

Effective time management is a talent that can greatly increase output, lower stress levels, and foster a stronger sense of fulfilment in one's personal and professional life. The following outlines the main ideas for improving time management.

1. Evaluate how much time you spend now: To obtain a clear picture of how you spend your time, start by identifying activities that eat up time and are not useful.

2. Establish meaningful goals: Specify your long-term goals and divide them into doable activities. Sort your goals according to urgency and priority.

3. Create an effective schedule: Use tactics like time blocking, to-do lists, and planners to arrange your time and guarantee that activities are performed efficiently.

4. Establish productive work habits. To stay focused and organized, avoid procrastinating, block out distractions, and use time management tools and apps.

5. Increase productivity by using the 80/20 rule, often known as the P reto Principle, to rank tasks and concentrate on the most important ones. Employ techniques to improve your energy, motivation, focus, and concentration.

5. Maintain a work-life balance by setting limits, prioritizing self-care, and cultivating wholesome connections. Include leisure pursuits to unwind, replenish energy, and preserve well-being.

6. Overcome Time Management Barriers: Address typical barriers, including overcommitting, procrastination, perfectionism, distractions, and time limits. Use proven tactics and mindset modifications to overcome these problems.

7. Develop a management mindset: Take a growth-oriented approach, strengthen your discipline and resilience, and value ongoing development. For long-term

success, establish routines for time management and maintain constructive behaviours.

A person can become an expert time manager by adhering to these guidelines and using the suggested methods and approaches. Recall that efficient time management is about making the most of our time, not packing in extra hours for the day. Anybody can learn how to manage their time well and reap the reward of higher output, lower stress levels, and a more contented and balanced existence with practice and persistence.

When the workday is almost over, stop working.

Stopping work when the workday is over is one of the most crucial scheduling advice. This is equally as crucial as planning out your daily tasks. It will allow you to wind down and give you a clear schedule for the day. You'll be more likely to maintain a healthy work schedule if you set a specific time to stop working. Doing the remaining tasks on certain occasions rather than putting them off until the next day is okay. Do not let going of your work schedule become a habit.

A Work-from-home Schedule That Works

All of the topics covered so far in this chapter should be included in the ideal schedule. The specific times, however, will change based on when you start and end. Generally speaking, you should refrain from rising right before your shift is scheduled to begin. Although it could be tempting, doing this won't help you get started on a productive note in the morning. You'll stay awake much of the morning attempting to get back to sleep, so it will take you considerably longer to get into the weekday routine. I wanted to share an example of my daily plan with you to give you an idea of what a work-from-home routine should entail.

Early Morning Alert

Setting your alarm for a respectable hour in the morning is something you should do every time. This is approximately 7:30 a.m. for me. This allows me to complete my daily routine in plenty of time before my 9 a.m. work start time. This start time, though, is entirely up to you. Ensure you sleep for at least eight hours the previous night, and avoid setting your alarm to snooze.

Establish a Morning Routine

I devote the first hour of my waking hours to my morning ritual. Like many others, I often listen to audiobooks or podcasts along with my morning workout. I get a tremendous energy boost at the beginning of the day and can accomplish something worthwhile and learn. To ensure there are no distractions during the day, you can incorporate additional morning routines like yoga, meditation, reading the newspaper, or doing some housework if you don't enjoy it. Whatever you decide, make sure you follow through on it every day to establish a habit.

morning

I take pleasure in my daily coffee at 8:35 a.m. I use this time to reflect on the day ahead and my goals based on the plan I created the previous evening. You might prepare some meals for the next day or eat breakfast with your family during this time. Everything is dependent upon your schedule.

Get to Work

I start working at 9 a.m. I read my emails within the first hour of work to see whether any demand my quick attention. I find that this is a terrific way to start the day off well.

Verify cations

I check to see if I have any check-ins to do around roughly 10:15 a.m. I will make my calls, plan the week's meetings, and submit reports at this time. I use that time to spend with people before I settle down to work for the day.

Returning to Work

I set aside this time to focus on my work throughout this period. It ranges between an hour or two, depending on how long it takes me to finish my previous check-ins. I put my phone aside and concentrated on the tasks I had set during this time to prevent distractions.

Remind Yourself to Hydrate

Working from home can indeed cause you to lose track of time. Reminders to stay hydrated and drink water are a terrific way to break the day into small segments. I prefer to take one in the morning at 11:30 a.m. since I know that I tend to become overwhelmed with work. We frequently overlook the significance of maintaining proper hydration, and drinking coffee won't cut it.

During lunch

Normally, I take a lunch break at 12:30 p.m. I will step away from my workstation for around 45 minutes. I'll make lunch or go to the local deli for a quick week. Because of this, I can take a much-needed break and start over for the afternoon.

Afternoon Schedule

I return to my workspace and resume my afternoon schedule as soon as I return to work. Sometimes, when I feel like losing energy, I take my laptop and find a different place to sit. I understand that not everyone can do this, but even a small change of scenery might cheer you up.

Human-Human Relations

I check in with a couple of coworkers who work from home at about 2:30 p.m. This allows me to socialize a little, even if I do not work in an office. Connecting with coworkers who struggle with loneliness when working from home is also beneficial.

Pause

I then go outside for a little walk around three o'clock in the afternoon. Those who prefer not to work out in the morning could alternatively plan their workout for this time. When it comes to the afternoon slump that many professionals have, his time helps.

Observation

I use the time after my afternoon break to review the work I did during the day and ensure my desk is organized for the following day. While it doesn't take long, doing this will make it easier for you to start the next day.

Organizing

I schedule my duties for the following day during the period that follows my afternoon reflection. At approximately five o'clock in the evening, I review my schedule and add anything missing. I routinely review my weekly targets to ensure I am on track to reach my productivity target.

Day's End

I turn off my computer at 6:30 p.m. and leave my workspace. I can now finish my workday and enjoy my time since I have the necessary mental and physical distance.

Your schedule doesn't need to work at the same times every day. All it needs to do is adhere to a schedule that suits you.

Never forget that you can make a schedule as long or short as you choose. All it needs to do is provide your brain with the regularity and structure to stay productive and practice the crucial time management skills required to achieve your personal and professional objectives.

Allocate time for physical activity.

Exercise is essential to any single mother's self-care regimen for her physical and emotional wellbeing. Some may claim that it's difficult to find time for exercise with many obligations and time restrictions. But even 15 minutes a day of physical activity can have significant advantages that make it well worth the time and effort.

Frequent exercise helps you stay physically fit and is also essential for strengthening your overall attractiveness and self-confidence. Your mood is naturally elevated by the endorphins released during physical activity, which can help you cope with the day-to-day stressors of being a single mother.

Furthermore, it has been demonstrated that exercise is a useful strategy for controlling and lowering anxiety and depressive symptoms, which are frequently made worse by the responsibilities of single parenting.

The dilemma is how a single mother can fit exercise into her already hectic day. A gym membership is one thing to think about, ideally one that provides child care. This way, you may exercise without the added worry of finding a babysitter and have the peace of mind to check on your child whenever needed during your workout.

Several options are accessible for people on a tight budget, from inexpensive exercise plans to free online video courses. All you need is a mat, some comfy exercise attire, and ten to fifteen extra minutes during your child's sleep or before they get up in the morning.

You not only invest in your health and happiness when you prioritize exercise as a crucial component of your self-care routine; you also provide a good example for your child, highlighting the significance of taking care of oneself despite life's obstacles.

Spend time doing the things you enjoy.

It is simple to forget who you are and that life is about more than just getting by each day when you take on the position of primary caregiver for your kids full-time.

It won't take long for you to feel completely exhausted in this condition, both mentally and physically. Making time for fun and relaxation becomes essential to avoiding the burnout that single mothers frequently experience.

For mothers amidst the chaos of single parenthood, self-care can take many forms, from making a small adjustment to bedtime to taking up novel creative pursuits like blogging.

Shut your eyes for a moment and try to picture what you would do if you had everything in the world to yourself.

Maybe it's taking a warm bath with scented candles, losing yourself in a good book, taking care of a colourful flower garden, or doing anything else that makes you happy.

These pastimes and interests are vital for preserving your sanity and rejuvenating your mental faculties, not only for brief moments of escape.

You'll notice that you become less agitated and impatient if you often take your mind off the never-ending responsibilities of parenting. Prioritizing self-care is a way to ensure you are ready to be the best mother you can be for your child and take care of your well-being. It is not selfishness.

Remember, in the bustle of single parenting, spending time for yourself is not a luxury; it's a need.

Procedure For Putting The Selected Strategy Into Action

Planning, dedication, and adaptability are necessary when implementing a time management approach. This procedure typically entails the following steps, though it may differ based on the chosen approach and specific needs:

1. Context analysis and self-awareness: These two are the first and most important steps in putting any time management plan into practice. Knowing your requirements, preferences, strengths and limitations regarding time management is essential. Selecting the best course of action can be aided by clearly understanding your

work habits, peak productivity periods, and break requirements. Consider your personal and professional lives as well. Each of these factors will impact your time management.

2. Strategy formulation: After assessing your circumstances and selecting a course of action, it is necessary to begin forming it. For example, if you have chosen to use the Pomodoro Technique, you must schedule your time in 25-minute blocks and take quick five-minute breaks. If you have opted for the Time Slot Method, however, you will have to pinpoint the times of the day that you may set apart for particular chores. You will also set specific goals and objectives in this stage that you

hope to accomplish using your time management plan.

3. Training and preparation: You must put yourself in the greatest possible position to succeed, regardless of your approach. This could entail studying more material, utilizing timers or tracking apps, and practising the methods before applying them completely. By getting ready, you can also spot possible roadblocks to your plan and plan how to get around them.

4. Strategy Implementation: This is the stage in which you carry out all your preparations. Keep a log of your time on each activity during this phase. This will assist you in determining whether your

plan is effective or changes need to be made.

5. Assessment and improvement: It's critical to assess the success of your time management plan after you've put it into practice. Are you meeting your targets and goals? Do you feel less stressed and more productive? You might need to modify your approach if any of these questions have a negative response. Constantly improving your time management plan is necessary to keep it working.

It's critical to remember that putting any time management approach into practice involves a process. Don't anticipate outcomes right away. Real progress is attained by persistence, flexibility, and a readiness to change and advance. A good time management technique changes your requirements and makes you more productive and happier.

These implementation process steps each lay a strong foundation for you to take charge of your time. By doing this, you can raise your level of productivity while also enhancing your happiness and contentment in all facets of your life. Finally, remember that everyone is unique and that what suits one person may not suit another. Thus, don't be scared to try different approaches until you identify the one that suits you best.

Overcoming challenges during the execution phase

The road to efficient time management is not simple; rather, it is paved with curves, detours, and unforeseen difficulties. It is imperative to learn how to go beyond these obstacles if you want to succeed. In this part, we'll talk about overcoming challenges while putting time management techniques into practice.

First and foremost, it is critical to realize that every person will have distinct challenges because of their personal and work environments. Early detection of these challenges will enable you to better prepare for them and create workable backup plans.

One of the most frequent challenges people face is resistance to change. Even positive changes can cause worry and anxiety, making it difficult to implement new time management techniques. To overcome this obstacle, it can be useful to remember that any change—no matter how minor—may call for a period of adjustment. If initially you don't get results right away, don't worry. Allow yourself to learn and adapt at the speed that suits you best, and practice self-compassion.

The absence of other people's support could be another obstacle. It's possible that some people in your immediate vicinity don't see how important your new time management technique is, and their inflated expectations could put you under needless stress. Communicating your intentions and outlining how these adjustments will benefit you—and them—can help you get over this obstacle. Seek assistance from internet networks or interest groups that share your time management objectives.

Discipline issues are yet another problem people encounter while trying out new tactics. It's simple to revert to old behaviours, particularly in difficult or stressful circumstances. This is the point at which individual dedication is necessary. Remember your objectives, and never forget why you began this trip. Reward minor victories, and don't punish yourself for failures. No matter how tiny, every step counts toward your final objective.

The obstacle of improper implementation could also appear. You run the risk of using time management techniques improperly and getting subpar outcomes if you don't thoroughly understand how they operate. To get beyond this obstacle, be sure you comprehend every tactic completely before employing it.

And last, a major barrier may be demotivation. Effective time management takes time, and it can be hard to stay motivated if you don't see results right away. Always remember to recognize and appreciate your little successes. Every activity you complete successfully indicates that you are making progress. You might also journal your accomplishments to stay motivated and remind yourself of your progress.

While overcoming these challenges may seem overwhelming, it is not insurmountable. Recall that managing your time is a personal and distinct process and that it's acceptable to run into obstacles along the road. These challenges present chances for growth and improvement along your route to efficient time management.

Overcoming challenges while putting time management techniques into practice calls for tolerance, dedication, comprehension, and, most of all, tenacity. These challenges are a typical aspect of change, and you can successfully overcome them and meet your time management objectives if you have an optimistic outlook and are prepared to adapt and learn.

Last but not least, it's critical to acknowledge and thank yourself for all your accomplishments, no matter how tiny. This can keep you inspired and increase the enjoyment of your work.

Rewarding yourself is a crucial part of motivation and self-care. It is beneficial to recognize and honour your accomplishments and endeavours, and it can inspire you to keep pursuing your objectives. Self-rewarding can take numerous forms, and the one that suits you the most may vary depending on your tastes and situation.

Treating yourself to something you enjoy, like your favourite meal or pastime, is one way to reward yourself. This might be as easy as having a soothing bubble bath or enjoying a scoop of your favourite ice cream. It might also involve something more lavish, like planning a weekend trip or treating yourself to a new technology.

Making time for oneself is another way to treat yourself. This could entail planning a day at the spa, enrolling in a yoga class, or just reading or practising meditation in peace. You may refuel and rejuvenate by making time for yourself, increasing your motivation and productivity in daily life.

You can also reward yourself by making progress towards a goal. For instance, you may treat yourself to a vacation or buy a new item you've been eyeing if you've been working hard to save money. Alternatively, if you've been working on a challenging project, you may treat yourself to a day off or a nice supper with friends. You may feel more proud of your efforts and accomplishments as a result.

Returning the favour by helping others is another way to treat yourself. This can be accomplished by lending a hand to a friend or relative in need, volunteering, or donating. You may feel more fulfilled and purposeful as a result, and you may also learn to value the positive aspects of your life.

Whatever approach you decide, it's critical to remember that doing something that makes you feel good is the secret to rewarding yourself. It ought to be something you enjoy and feel proud of yourself for. It's also critical to keep in mind to treat yourself regularly. Celebrate your little victories; don't save self-indulgence for a major accomplishment. Rewarding yourself regularly will help you stay motivated and goal-focused.

In summary, self-rewarding plays a critical role in motivation and self-care. It is beneficial to recognize and honour your accomplishments and endeavours, and it can inspire you to keep pursuing your objectives. Rewarding oneself can take various forms: it can be as simple as giving yourself something you enjoy, scheduling time for yourself, achieving a goal, or contributing to the community. Whichever approach you choose, never forget to regularly treat yourself to something enjoyable.

Through adherence to these guidelines and ongoing introspection, people can employ self-regulation as a useful tool for goal attainment.

Chapter 3: Unlock Your Potential: Methods for Developing Yourself

Developing oneself to a higher level is a process that can be accomplished in several ways. It's taking charge of your life and consciously trying to better yourself. There are numerous methods to improve yourself, whether your goals are relationships, profession, or general happiness.

Enhancing oneself via personal development is among the best strategies to start. This can involve reading books, attending seminars or workshops, and looking for coaching or mentoring. You can get important perspectives, abilities, and knowledge from these activities that will aid in your understanding of the world and yourself. They can also assist you in finding direction and a feeling of purpose, which can be immensely powerful.

Taking care of oneself is another crucial component of elevating oneself. This can entail consistent exercise, a balanced diet, adequate rest, and constructive stress management. You can increase your general energy and mood by taking care of yourself, making you more successful and productive in all facets of your life.

Setting objectives for yourself and taking charge of your life are other aspects of elevating oneself. This may entail creating a strategy for reaching short- and long-term objectives. Setting attainable objectives and holding oneself responsible for your accomplishments are crucial. You might feel more in control of your life and experience pleasure and success when you set and accomplish goals.

Lastly, developing solid and encouraging relationships is another aspect of uplifting oneself. Have helpful and encouraging individuals in your life, be they friends, family, or love partners. Developing solid relationships can also aid in developing a sense of belonging and community, which are highly beneficial to your emotional and mental well-being.

To sum up, improving yourself is a lifetime endeavour that calls for commitment and diligence. One can accomplish this process of personal growth and development in several ways. You may improve yourself and have a happier, more fulfilled life by emphasizing goal-setting, self-care, personal growth, and forming solid relationships.

Practicing Mindfulness And Managing One's Thoughts

As we explore the topics of mindfulness and mind management, I cordially ask you to join me on a life-changing adventure. This chapter invites readers to embrace the power of clear thinking, cultivate a peaceful and focused mind, and live in the present. It is more than just words on a page. If you apply these skills, your life will become a harmonious symphony of presence, focus, and discernment.

In the modern world, when an endless stream of data, alerts, and assignments compete for our attention, mindfulness and mental hygiene are more important than ever. In this fast-paced day, where being constantly connected is praised and time is frequently associated with work, mindfulness appears as a ray of hope and reason.

Think of this chapter as a quiet haven in the digital chaos. Imagine entering a tranquil garden where the sound of running water and the soft rustle of leaves remain as the outside world fades away. Here's where you can recover mental clarity, regain control of your thoughts, and intentionally focus your attention: the field of mindfulness and mind management.

Embracing mindfulness means more than just starting a self-improvement path; it's about adopting a way of life that enhances every aspect of your life. Remove layers of distraction and cultivate a strong connection to the present moment by practising mindfulness.

The techniques described in this chapter counter a society that frequently exalts multitasking and being perpetually occupied. They allow you to slowly disconnect from the deluge of outside stimuli and take in life's richness without being overwhelmed by its demands.

Let's examine the amazing advantages of implementing mindfulness exercises into your daily routine, cultivate a quiet, concentrated mind, and discover how to employ mental clarity to inform your decisions. Adopting these routines will help you live a more deliberate and present life and plant the seeds of significant personal development and fulfilment.

Welcome to the world of mind control and mindfulness, where mastering the skill of being is just as important as mastering the art of doing.

Including Mindfulness Exercises in Everyday Life:

Take a moment to relax and open your thoughts. See every day as a blank canvas ready to be filled with the colours of mindfulness. Imagine being fully present and paying attention to all of life's moments, big and small. Skin or the comforting warmth of your morning cup of tea—mindfulness offers a fresh perspective. It seems like you're waking up to a symphony of feelings that have been there in the background for a while, just waiting for you to recognize and enjoy them.

Mindfulness weaves the needle of intention in the tapestry of your daily life, helping you completely engage with every stitch, fibre, and moment. It's the practice of living intentionally—a deliberate act of appreciating, relishing, and cherishing each moment, no matter how big or small. A contemplative cup of tea becomes a meditation; a leisurely walk becomes an awareness trip.

Bringing mindfulness into your everyday existence is like adding a little enchantment to the everyday. It's about discovering your true nature again, being in tune with your breathing, and becoming more experiences constantly flowing through you. Mindfulness provides a calm haven in the middle of life's hectic bustle—a place of peace where you can find comfort even amid turmoil.

The Practice of Mindful Pausing

As you take the first steps towards integrating mindfulness into your everyday routine, I'm here to offer you a vital tool: the Mindful Pause. Even though it's a simple exercise, it has the power to significantly alter your life. It's an invitation to open the door to the abundance of presence hidden in every moment you have.

Select a Trigger: Choose a regular event in your day, such as opening a door, getting a notification, or eating your first mouthful. This is what will set off your Mindful Pause.

Take a moment to breathe: Consciously stop when the selected trigger happens. Permit yourself to inhale deeply and mindfully.

Involve Your Senses:

Pay attention to the environment around you.

Take note of the surrounding hues, patterns, and noises.

Take full advantage of your senses and thoroughly immerse yourself in the present.

Take Stock of Yourself: Gently scan your body and mind. What bodily state are you in? Which feelings are there? Be observant without passing judgment.

Proceed Mindfully: Now, maintain this mindful awareness while you carry out the remainder of your task. With purpose, approach the task, giving each step your whole attention.

By engaging in the Mindful Pause periodically during the day, you can elevate the ordinary to the remarkable. It's a simple reminder that you can bring awareness, intention, and a little magic into your life. May you find the beauty of being present in every aspect of your path as you begin this practice.

Organizing Meetings Effectively

We have now discussed when it is proper to call a meeting. It's time to assess how to get the most out of one now. It is better to have a one-hour meeting with a smooth discussion of the entire agenda than two hours with only half of the findings completed. However, many leaders overlook the significance of having a defined agenda when organizing. Consider the subjects to be covered as more than just a list of words. Instead, ask them a question. Answering the question, "Under what circumstances should project resources be reallocated?" is a simple task for your team. However, a message like "Project Resources and Reallocations" could indicate many different things. Your friend is specific!

Make sure the folks you invite are the most appropriate. Large meetings are appealing, but regulating eight speakers is simpler and more efficient than controlling twenty. In the same spirit, include subjects that impact all attendees. When you do, ascertain the purpose of every subject. Are you seeking input on a choice you've made? Or are you trying to find answers? Put this goal and other useful information on your agenda. This can contain any reading material that everyone has to catch up on before the event, or it can list which team member—if not you—is in charge of each topic.

In keeping with these last ideas, be receptive to input from your group. Ask them to suggest things for the agenda. Inquire as to the significance of the item in question and discuss whether it relates to the meeting. Accept responsibility if it doesn't. Inform your teammates of your choice and the rationale behind its omission. In certain cases, it might be a significant topic but not one that many people will find sufficiently relevant. When you do this, take the initiative and point your teammates in the direction of alternative discussion topics if you think they should be covered.

When at all feasible, try to accommodate your team's schedule. This will make it possible for the most significant guests to attend. Make sure that the questions and conclusions are compiled into a brief summary that can be accessed by anyone who was unable to attend as a backup plan. Finally, and maybe most crucially, figure out how much time is required for each topic. It's simple to state that it will take fifteen minutes, even if it means that eleven employees would have to rush to come to a decision after speaking for about a minute apiece. Though it won't be exact, the more times you complete this activity, the closer your estimate will become to the real one.

As the host, you have a lot of influence over the direction that your meetings go. Therefore, effective facilitation can prevent a meeting from going longer than necessary. We have already discussed several pre-meeting actions that should be helpful, but keep time in mind. As the host, your goal is to let everyone contribute as much as they can without going over schedule. Give them some practice speaking clearly. To put it briefly, to stay precise, succinct, and relevant. Teach them to listen with patience and attention and without passing judgment. Make every effort to ensure that each participant has a stake in and accountability for at least one topic. This will not only keep everyone focused, but it will also facilitate a more cohesive meeting.

Remember each agenda item's procedure and substance when you are facilitating. Every issue has a what and a how. Notifying attendees of this information ahead of time can help save time and ensure they know what to expect. These may be recommendations from you or straight from the subject matter experts for each area. It will be your responsibility as a mediator to ensure that these procedures are followed. Using deltas to conclude my meetings has also helped them become less intimidating and more effective. Get input from your team regarding the organization and flow of the meeting. Was there anything in particular that was successful? What other options are they interested in trying at the next meetings?

Allowing a trainee to compile a minute is also a smart idea. This frees up important staff members from writing so they may concentrate solely on speaking and listening. Additionally, this will be a fantastic chance for you to teach your new hire the principles of management. Make sure it feels like a mentoring, not a chore.

This brings me to my next point nicely. Ensure that every duty is delegated and understood. It's one of the important aspects that your minutes should contain. This will make following up through chat or email a lot easier. Getting an employee up to speed is especially crucial if they were assigned a task but weren't present. Similar to how we prioritize our own schedules, it's polite to allow others to maintain their organization. Take the time to explain the work and its measurements if there are any questions. In the long run, this will save you more time than it will cost.

Whilst managing a project, be transparent. Being accountable is a two-way street. It goes without saying that you should be truthful with your supervisor, but it can be even more crucial to assume accountability for your team. We should strive to communicate clearly by without withholding anything. Transparency fosters distrust, but transparency fosters cooperation.

Chapter 8: Outsourcing and Delegation

Assigning

Recognize your worth.

"If you could take the tasks that you are currently doing and just do them all day, every day, and what would the impact be?" asked one of my old mentors. "What would they be and what would the impact be upon your business in terms of profit and turnover?"

These were sage remarks!

My business took off as soon as I began to only take on assignments that were equal to or more than my hourly rate, assigning the remaining work to others.

With regard to SME owners, the same is true.

Many small and medium-sized business owners believe that outsourcing or "letting go" of particular duties raises their overhead. Yes, it does increase the cost base, but in terms of turnover and profits, what would an extra 80% of you doing what you do best bring to your company? For small and medium-sized business owners, the ability to delegate duties effectively is essential since it directly contributes to time management. Despite assigning nearly every task that comes their way, some small business owners still have a severe time crunch.

SME owners typically have a "take charge" mentality. They are experts in their fields and are capable of handling almost any task. These entrepreneurs typically refuse to let go of jobs below their competence, which is not always in the best interest of the organization. These owners cling to tasks like if the captain of the ship refused to give up swabbing the deck because he believed no one could swab a deck like him. Many a corporate vessel has run aground with spotless decks.

You have to make decisions as a small business owner about which tasks are best left to in-house staff or outside vendors. Give up any obligations that might be better left to others.

Although they may approach the task differently than you, some people may nevertheless accomplish the same goals.

Question every task in front of you. Determine who, aside from you, could execute each one.

If you find this challenging, try to picture yourself if you could only delegate. Who would take up your duties?

Whenever feasible, offer staff options. Let them choose the responsibilities they want to take on.

If there are employees who may be more skilled in a particular area, think about assigning jobs to each other.

Recall that delegation ought to provide you with more time. There is a thin line separating effective delegation and incompetence on the part of others. Give motivated staff members the chance to try out new tasks, but don't assign them jobs that are too difficult for them to do. For ambitious personnel, think about initiating or funding educational or training initiatives.

Be careful about distributing a task among persons. Putting people in groups could lead to new problems with human management, negating any time savings.

Communicate deadlines and expectations for assigned work in an effective manner.

Checklist of Tasks Assigned

- Write Out Your Task Plan and Track Your Progress
- Clearly state your objective. Ensure that the individual or individuals comprehend the intended outcomes.
- Draw a drawing that illustrates the desired result.
- Choose the parameters for the outcome analysis.
- Make the outcomes quantifiable.
- Ascertain what challenges delegates would face, including financial constraints, scheduling issues, etc.
- Make a list of the steps you must take to accomplish your objective. Jot down as many thoughts as you can.

- Establish task milestones and provide high priority to the most important and productive actions.
- Make instructions as easy to follow as you can.
- Regularly go over the action plan. If you learn anything new, include it in your plan by making adjustments.
- Keep an eye on the tasks assigned. Establish task benchmarks and invite others to report back to you on progress at key junctures.

When assigned tasks don't get finished or yield unfavourable outcomes, try to have a backup plan.

Contracting out

Numerous small-business owners have realized the advantages of outsourcing, including accounting services and projects. For any project or service, consideration must be given to the amount of time needed to find suppliers, verify references, assess offerings, gather quotes, and arrange payment.

Is It Urgent Or Just Important?

It should not be too difficult for you to determine what is necessary.

The activity in the last chapter helped you arrange and prioritize your chores effectively. Since this is a private topic that differs from person to person, it is impossible to gauge relevance in this context. It matters if it resonates with your basic values and the tenets that guide your life.

Conversely, if anything needs your quick attention, then it's urgent.

If you want to manage your time effectively, you must be aware of this distinction. Remember that not everything important is urgent and that not everything vital is either.

Case A above was an easy decision because you valued the call, and it was urgent. For the safety and well-being of a dear one, an immediate decision needs to be taken; something is at stake (or appears to be, and you wouldn't take a chance on anything like that).

Everything important and urgent in life operates similarly. Even if it asks a lot of us, it doesn't make any decisions for us.

Case C, the discussion regarding your relationship, is equally important, but depending on your viewpoint, it might not seem urgent (why now?) or even inappropriate (not now!).

Because Case B is farther away from your SO and involves the unlucky Carol and Bobby in Oregon, it seems less urgent and considerably less vital.

The case with the least sense of urgency is D.

You should justify your selections for a good reason—possibly even urgently. B and C, or "urgent but not important" and "important but not urgent," respectively, are the categories that most of us struggle with. Specifically, you may be paying too much attention to the Cs and not enough attention to the Bs.

Posing the "Want to/Have to" dilemma

If all this business of classifying tasks into four quadrants on an important/urgent grid seems like a lot of effort, that's okay; there is a simpler method to begin taking charge of your everyday life. Again, you'll have to figure out a way to interrupt yourself several times daily. These pauses may be associated with

They don't have to be brief getaways for you. Just stop what you're doing, take a moment to breathe, and pose these questions to yourself:

"Do I need to or want to be doing this right now? (This version was developed by adapting Alan Lakein's 1973 book "Lakein Question"). However, don't forget to include these three essential elements:

Do I desire this?

Or give me a call

to be engaged right now?

You'll notice it says "or," not "and." Even if a job is vital, it may differ entirely from what you would prefer to do. If "yes" answers this question, return to your previous task. Deliberate decision-making, which you will have demonstrated by confirming your selection of activities, is essential to time management. Put it off if you don't want to or can't accomplish it right now.

Pay more attention to the timing of your actions. This way.

Later on, you won't be under deadline strain.

If you don't need to or want to stop, stop doing it now and forever!

If you ask yourself the "want/need" question frequently, you'll start to observe yourself acting in ways you know you shouldn't be doing. This may seem unbelievable to you.

Adjusting operations to more efficiently satisfy your needs.

This simple question can make a big difference in your life.

Recognizing When Time Is Not the Problem

To finish the image, we must underline this point once more:

Time management involves more than just time.

It's far easier to doze off than to work out, even though attending that departmental meeting while dozing off is not important or fun (unless you have a talent for daydreaming).

Many of us might feel that meeting the deadline at work is far easier than smoothing over the knots in our relationships. Most of the time, we will take the least difficult path if we can justify our choice with factors other than convenience. (I must depart for the conference.)

The Reasons You Can't Ever "Find" Time

Time needs to be "managed" only because it seems we never have enough time to complete everything. In particular, it seems we never "find time" for the tasks that are necessary but not urgent. Give up looking. You'll never have time. Nothing has vanished. It is a part of you. You must make a conscious decision to practice it in certain ways and not others. Time is something you have to create by shifting it from one work to another.

If the to-do list is applied intelligently and imaginatively, it can be useful. If you want to work out three times a week, if you need to plan your long-term career and finances, or if you value your relationship with someone enough to want to cultivate it, you will set aside time for these activities. If not, you may never "get to them," and even if you do, you'll simply be spending your leftover time with them when your energy and focus are at their lowest.

You may make more time for the important things in life by focusing less on the items in the last category—the "neither important nor urgent" group. You shouldn't eliminate this category, either those we partake in for fun or coincidental reasons.

Chapter 12: In-Depth Work

The capacity to concentrate intently on a single subject at a time is becoming more and more uncommon in today's fast-paced world. It can be challenging to focus on a single job for an extended period when we are constantly distracted by our phones, emails, and social media updates. This is where the idea of "deep work" is relevant.

In his book of the same name, Cal Newport defines deep work as the capacity to concentrate undistractedly on a subject that requires a lot of cognitive labour. In an increasingly mechanized society, shallow work—jobs that are simple to duplicate and demand little mental effort—becomes more and more lucrative.

Deep work is a concept that can be divided into multiple phases:

Step 1: Reducing Interruptions

Reducing distractions is essential to achieving deep work. This entails locating a quiet workspace free from interruptions, shutting down any tabs on your computer, and turning off your phone. Establishing a distraction-free workplace is crucial if you want to concentrate entirely on the subject at hand.

Step 2: Establishing Objectives

It's time to establish specific objectives for your deep work session after you've removed all distractions. This entails determining precisely what you hope to achieve in your concentrated work period. Setting clear, quantifiable goals will help you monitor your progress and maintain motivation.

Step 3: Establishing a Custom

Establishing a ritual that tells your brain when to focus can help you get into a deep state of work. This might be as easy as brewing tea or putting on a particular song. The goal is to establish a reliable schedule that signals your brain when it's time to concentrate.

Step 4: Acknowledging Boredom

The boredom that might result from concentrating on a single task for an extended period is one of the main obstacles to serious work. Embracing this dullness and pushing through it is more crucial than giving in to the need to take a break or check your phone. You may reach a deep state of focus and get more done in less time if you force yourself to push through the boredom.

Step 5: Taking Intervals

Even if deep work necessitates prolonged concentration, taking breaks is crucial to refuel and prevent burnout. This might be as simple as going for a short walk, stretching, or spending a few minutes away from your desk. You can maintain your focus for longer if you take regular rests.

When engaging in deep labour, it's critical to remember that time equals money. You can do more in less time by devoting yourself to meaningful work, which can help you succeed personally and professionally. Purchasing resources and tools that aid concentration, like noise-cancelling headphones or a dedicated workspace, can also be a smart approach to "buy back your time" and boost output.

Take, for instance, the narrative of a well-known writer who produced a best-selling book by applying intense concentration. She realized that her usual writing schedule, which included frequent interruptions from email and social media, did not help generate excellent work. She decided to put in a lot of effort and dedicated several hours a day to writing just. Her manuscript became a blockbuster and catapulted her to even greater fame because she removed all distractions and dedicated herself to intense effort.

To sum up, deep work is useful for anyone trying to reach their objectives and increase productivity. You may establish a distraction-free atmosphere and reach a deep level of focus by following the steps listed above, which will enable you to get more done in less time. Recall that time is money and making significant investments.

Effective Communication

Navigating change requires effective communication. Maintain communication with your team, particularly if you're working remotely. Use technology to keep everyone informed and involved, such as email, Slack, or video calls. These can help you build solid relationships.

Think about a marketing company that made the switch to remote work. They created a feeling of community, promoted open communication, and preserved a strong team culture by utilizing virtual communication technologies. They were able to adjust to change and become more creative and productive due to this technique.

Gain Resilience

Although adapting to change can be difficult, doing so will help you stay composed and on task. Here are some methods for honing this essential ability:

Recognize that life and business are full of change.

To assist in the processing of emotions, express your thoughts and feelings.

Determine which areas of change you have influence over and which you do not. Pay attention to what you can control and ask for help or guidance when unsure.

In summary, accepting change necessitates resilience, an optimistic outlook, good communication, and goal reevaluation. By implementing these tactics, you and your group can find chances for development and achievement in addition to adjusting to new problems.

Acquiring Knowledge From Errors

Acknowledging that making errors is an inherent aspect of being human is critical. Normally, mistakes or setbacks will periodically occur for you and your staff as remote work becomes more popular. Nonetheless, these occurrences can provide insightful teaching moments that result in enhanced decision-making and professional partnerships.

To effectively learn from your mistakes, take the following actions:

Step 1: Own Up to Your Mistakes

Demonstrate real remorse and take responsibility for your errors. By being open and honest with your coworkers, you can establish confidence in your professional relationships by demonstrating that the error was accidental.

Step 2: Recognize the Primary Cause

Determine what went wrong, why it happened, and how to keep it from happening again. For instance, if you didn't send a crucial report because it wasn't scheduled, ensure you are better prepared by keeping careful track of your assignments and due dates.

Step 3: Request Input

Speak with supervisors and coworkers to get their advice on going forward and steer clear of past mistakes. Positive feedback can help people advance both personally and professionally.

Step 4: Look for the bright side

Every negative experience presents a chance for growth. You can make a bad circumstance into a worthwhile learning experience by realizing where you went wrong and how to prevent making the same mistakes again.

Step5: Use the Knowledge Acquired

Put the techniques and answers you've found into practice to stop making the same mistakes. Make sure you apply these skills to your everyday routine to achieve sustained progress.

Step 6: Give Your Knowledge Away

Share your knowledge with your coworkers to foster a culture of growth and learning. Through a collaborative discussion of typical mistakes, your team may effectively prevent and resolve them.

Step 7: Engage in Self-Examination

Evaluate your activities, successes, and lessons gained on a regular basis. You can identify your progress through this self-examination process, which also highlights how crucial it is to take lessons from your experiences.

Step 8: Welcome Ongoing Education

Remain receptive to new experiences and eager to learn from all of them, good and bad. Having this mentality will enable you to learn from your mistakes fast and keep them from negatively impacting your mental health.

By putting these strategies into practice, you'll be better able to grow from errors and form a resilient, flexible team that is prepared to take on the difficulties of a changing work environment.

Developing an Organizational Culture of Open Change

Establishing a culture of transparency and flexibility is essential for leaders to successfully manage change, particularly in light of the increasing popularity of remote work. The following tactics can assist you in creating a more accepting and flexible change culture in your company:

Accept Openness

Show your team that you are aware of and willing to deal with the feelings and difficulties that come with change. Your staff will look to you for direction and inspiration if you are prepared to talk candidly about your own experiences.

Remain dependable and comforting.

Make sure your staff members are aware that you will assist and mentor them during impending adjustments. They will feel secure in the face of uncertainty, knowing that you are willing to support them as they adjust and grow.

Set an Example and Provide Information

Inform your staff of impending changes that will affect their working environments. In addition to building trust, transparency makes workers feel prepared and involved in creating a culture that is flexible to change.

Provide Tailored Assistance

Acknowledge that staff members have varying learning curves and could need customized support to adjust to changes. Take the time to check in with each team member, and when needed, offer individualized direction and inspiration.

Deal with Opposition

Find out who might be undermining change initiatives by disseminating negativity or false information, and take appropriate action against them. You can reassure your employees and preserve a positive work atmosphere by promptly resolving such situations.

Take A Hint from Effective Remote Teams

Consult with companies that have successfully embraced remote work to get best practices and suggestions. Invest in technologies and tactics that promote efficient communication without being unduly controlling, as it is frequently stated that effective communication is a critical component of remote team success.

Encourage Responsibility and Accountability

Motivate your staff to accept responsibility for their job and to see the advantages of working remotely, such as a better work-life balance. Remind them that although you are there to help and mentor them, they still have accountability for their choices and behaviours.

Put into Practice and Refine

Remember that the process of switching to a new system is an iterative one. To develop a successful remote work environment, keep improving your approach and learning from your mistakes.

You'll be well-equipped to promote an open change culture that values cooperation and adaptation if you adhere to these tactics. This will guarantee that, despite upcoming problems, your business maintains its agility and resilience.

Acquiring Knowledge From Errors

The value of taking lessons from errors when it comes to time management
Large or small, mistakes are an unavoidable part of life. We all make

mistakes when managing our time when we strive to be productive and efficient. It's critical to remember that making mistakes is not the end of the world; rather, they present a priceless chance for growth and learning.

To begin with, let's define what constitutes a time management error. It's possible that we misjudged the time required to do a task, which led to tension and last-minute effort, or missed a crucial appointment because of work overload. Regardless of its nature, what counts is how we respond to the error.

We frequently react with anger or disappointment when we make a mistake. We may place the blame on external factors or ourselves, which can start a vicious cycle of negativity. But after we move past the initial emotional phase, we have a fantastic chance to reflect on what transpired and draw conclusions.

First, time management errors are a mirror, a crystal-clear representation of our shortcomings and potential growth areas. Although initially uncomfortable, this is a necessary step in our development as individuals and professionals. We can spot patterns and trends in our time management that can be causing inefficiency if we examine our errors with objectivity.

For instance, we might observe that we make mistakes more often in the afternoon, which could mean we are scheduling crucial work for when we are tired. Alternatively, we may find that attempting to manage too many things at once leads to mistakes, indicating that we need to work on our prioritization techniques.

Second, resilience is created through learning from mistakes. It is an essential life skill. We get the chance to put this ability to use when we make a time management error. We can learn to control the frustration and worry accompanying making a mistake and develop original solutions to get back on track.

Furthermore, each time we overcome an error, we bolster our self-assurance to meet new obstacles. This building of self-confidence is vital and can have a good impact on all parts of our lives.

Third, we become more sympathetic and understanding of others when we learn from our mistakes. We can all learn from our mistakes and extend that same understanding to others when we allow ourselves to do so rather than punishing ourselves for them. This degree of empathy can improve our interpersonal and professional connections and foster a more understanding and cooperative workplace.

In conclusion, although making time management errors can be upsetting and frustrating, they also present a great chance for growth and learning. Not only will this ability enable us to better organize our time, but it will also help us develop personally and enhance every part of our lives.

How to use errors as opportunities for growth

Errors and setbacks are a given in time management, just like in life. Although many see these failures as obstacles to achievement, they are necessary for learning and development. Making the most of your mistakes is more important than trying to prevent them.

One of the most potent tools in your toolbox for efficient time management is the capacity to use a mistake as a teaching opportunity. However, how is this change made possible? Here, we go over how to use a mistake as a teaching moment.

1. Recognize and Accept the Error

Recognizing and accepting one's mistake is the first step towards learning from it. Many people tended to blame others for their faults or disregard them. But the first step in learning from our mistakes is acknowledging that we made them. In this process, being sincere and true to oneself is crucial. When something goes wrong, it's critical to own up to it, determine what went wrong, and take accountability.

2. Examine the Mistake

Analyzing the error as soon as it has been identified is essential. You can determine the series of choices or acts that resulted in the error by dissecting it. It's critical to consider what you could have done differently. Which signals or cautions did I disobey? A crucial step in this analytical process is reflection.

3. Learn from Your Errors

The metamorphosis starts with this phase. This is when, following a careful examination, you must decide what lessons you can learn from the error. Finding the lessons you can learn from that bad experience will help you turn it around and see it as positive. For these lessons to be implemented in the future, they must be applicable and tangible.

4. Put the Knowledge into Practice

Without application, learning is useless. After studying the lessons, you must apply what you have learned to your future actions and choices. This could entail shifting your attention to particular jobs or activities or adjusting to an ineffective time management plan.

5. Sustain Your Resilience

Sustaining resilience is the final phase. Acknowledging errors may be a challenging and sensitive process. It may include acknowledging and confronting our flaws. However, maintaining a positive attitude and encouraging a resilient mindset can be achieved by remembering that everyone makes mistakes and that the most crucial thing is learning from them.

It is imperative to stress that there is no shortcut or simple route to this process.

It takes an active and ongoing commitment to evaluate, learn, and develop to turn mistakes into chances for growth. The benefits of this approach, however, are priceless. It enables you to keep refining your time management techniques and fosters a growth mentality that is advantageous in all facets of life.

Therefore, even though errors can feel overwhelming at the time, their real value comes from the lessons they teach. Making a mistake is a way to get better at managing your time and a chance for development, enhancement, and education. Thus, remember that making a mistake improves your time management skills.

It takes ongoing learning and development to improve time management, and our best teachers are the mistakes we make. Thus, accept your errors and grow from them. You'll soon realize that these experiences will serve as stepping stones to your successful time management.

3.4 The Rule of Two Minutes

The rule was made popular by productivity expert and "Getting Things Done" author David Allen. This method can help you organize your to-do list, reduce procrastination, and handle tiny jobs more effectively.

This is how the Two-Minute Rule should be used:

1. Find quick tasks: Throughout the day, watch for jobs that can be finished in two minutes or less. These could be answering a fast email, picking up the phone, or organizing your workspace.

2. Act now: Finish these quick jobs immediately rather than putting them off or adding them to your list of things to do. Doing this will prevent the accumulation of small chores that, if neglected, can grow tedious and time-consuming.

3. Set higher priorities for larger projects: Use time blocking, time boxing, or the Pomodoro Technique to schedule things that take longer than two minutes

into your day based on their importance and urgency.

4. Create a habit: Apply the Two-Minute Rule regularly throughout the day to form a habit. Your overall productivity and time management will increase as you get more comfortable with acting quickly on tiny tasks.

5. Remain adaptable: Using your discretion and remaining flexible is crucial, even though the Two-Minute Rule can serve as a useful guideline. It could be more productive to put off the two-minute assignment until you've finished your high-priority task or deep work session.

You may effectively tackle little chores, decrease procrastination, and keep momentum throughout your day by implementing the Two-Minute Rule into your time management plan. Making the most of your available time is made possible by this method, which frees up more time and mental energy for larger, more significant tasks.

3.5 How to Prevent Burnout and Overwhelm

Overwhelming and burnout can stem from inadequate time management, excessive workload, or insufficient self-care. Identifying overwhelm and taking proactive measures to avoid burnout is critical for maintaining productivity and wellbeing. The following tactics can assist you in preventing burnout and overwhelm:

1. Your workload, priorities, and available resources should set achievable and appropriate goals. Steer clear of overly ambitious aspirations, as they may cause undue stress and feelings of failure.

2. Make self-care a priority by planning frequent pauses throughout the day and setting aside time for pursuits that enhance your physical, mental, and emotional health. Examples include exercise, meditation, pastimes, and quality time with loved ones.

3. Delegate and work together: If you feel overburdened by your workload, consider assigning tasks to others or working together as a team to divide the

weight. This can lessen your stress and help you manage your workload more skillfully.

4. Learn to say "no": Avoid overloading yourself with work and other obligations by establishing limits and turning down new assignments. Set firm boundaries and give top priority to the things that matter.

5. Tasks should be broken down into smaller, more manageable sections to avoid being overwhelmed and make complex projects more approachable, as was covered earlier in this chapter.

6. Create a routine: Create a daily schedule that promotes your wellbeing and productivity. This could be having a morning routine to establish the tone for

the day, having regular work hours, and having a regular bedtime to guarantee enough sleep.

7. Seek support: If you need emotional or practical help, don't hesitate to ask friends, family, or coworkers for help. Talking to people about your emotions and experiences can reduce stress and open your eyes to new possibilities.

8. Continually evaluate how stressed you are and notice any physical or emotional indicators of exhaustion. Should you observe that you're experiencing constant feelings of being overwhelmed, you might want to reassess your tasks, priorities, and self-care routines.

9. Be flexible and adaptive: Accept change and be ready to modify your

plans or objectives as necessary. Accept that obstacles and failures are a normal part of life and use them as chances for development.

By putting these methods into practice, you may lessen your risk of burnout and experience less overload. Sustaining productivity and general wellbeing requires striking a healthy balance between work and self-care.

Combine related tasks into a batch to reduce context switching.

Moving between tasks or context switching can majorly cause lost productivity. It can be time-consuming and psychologically taxing to shift our focus, recall where we left off, and adapt our thinking each time we move from one work to another. Context switching can be reduced by grouping related tasks in batches.

Batching is assembling related tasks into groups and finishing them all at once. For instance, you can set out a certain period, like the first hour of the workday or right before you leave the office, to answer emails rather than doing so throughout the day. Similarly, you can arrange a specific time block for phone calls rather than making them intermittently throughout the day.

You can focus on a single activity for longer periods by grouping related tasks, reducing the frequency with which you must transition between different sorts of work. By doing so, you may be able to lessen the mental strain that comes with changing contexts, boosting output and improving your work's calibre.

You can also make the most of your natural energy or rhythms by grouping related chores. For example, if you are more awake in the morning, use this time to concentrate on mentally taxing or creative projects that need your attention. However, if you have more time in the afternoon, you can use it to work on monotonous or administrative activities.

Creating a routine and gaining control over your weekday is another advantage of grouping related chores. You can lessen your sense of overload or disarray by being clear about what has to be done and when.

Organizing and setting priorities for your work is crucial to a successful batch implementation. Sort the many kinds of work you must accomplish and place them in related groups. Next, set up specified time slots in your calendar for every category, remembering to provide time for unforeseen assignments and breaks.

Still, it's critical to be adaptive and flexible. Not every day will proceed as planned; unforeseen obligations or crises can occur. Try to be careful of your time and make any required schedule adjustments to ensure you can finish important chores while batching related things together.

In summary, grouping related jobs can be useful for reducing context switching and raising output. You may take advantage of natural cycles, minimize the mental strain of switching between different types of work, and create a sense of routine and control over your workday by grouping comparable tasks. Batching can help you work more productively and efficiently with some forethought and adaptability, eventually producing superior results.

Give yourself and others reasonable deadlines.

Achieving goals and efficient time management require setting reasonable deadlines. Tasks are prioritized and given a sense of urgency when deadlines are met. Setting unattainable deadlines, however, can result in tension, exhaustion, and subpar output. To be effective, timelines need to be realistic and doable.

Determining what has to be done and breaking it down into smaller, more doable tasks is the first step in creating realistic timelines. You can begin assigning due dates to each assignment once you have a clear idea of what needs to be done. When establishing deadlines, it's crucial to consider the amount of work needed, the resources at hand, and any potential roadblocks or limitations.

You must be honest with yourself and others about what can be accomplished in a given amount of time to set reasonable deadlines. Refraining from overcommitting and doing too much work at once is critical. This may result in inflated expectations, which could then cause missed deadlines or subpar work.

Using the SMART framework is one way to create deadlines. SMART stands for Time-bound, Specific, Measurable, Achievable, and Relevant. Deadlines that are relevant to the overall objective, defined, and attainable are helped to ensure by this framework. It also gives a precise deadline for completion.

Precious and unambiguous deadlines define what needs to be done and by when. Measurable deadlines enable the tracking and measurement of progress because they are quantifiable. Given the resources at hand, achievable timelines are reasonable and doable. Deadlines pertinent to the task at hand support attaining the main objective. Last but not least, time-bound deadlines have a set amount of time to be completed.

Working with people is another way to create reasonable timelines. When working in a team, it's critical to have open and honest communication regarding deadlines. This entails determining reasonable timelines for all parties and accounting for the workloads and schedules of each participant. Working with others can help you ensure that deadlines are reasonable, reachable, and in keeping with the project's or team's overall objectives.

It's also critical to exercise flexibility when establishing due dates. One must be able to modify timelines in response to unforeseen circumstances and roadblocks. This builds wiggle room into your deadlines to account for unanticipated circumstances or delays. Being adaptable can help you finish projects on time without adding to the stress and strain of missing deadlines.

To summarise, realistic deadline setting is crucial to time management and goal achievement. By working with others and utilizing frameworks like SMART, You may ensure that deadlines are precise, quantifiable, attainable, pertinent, and time-bound. You may lower stress and improve your chances of success by being realistic about what can be accomplished and being honest with others and yourself about what is possible. You can also be adaptable when unforeseen circumstances arise. Setting reasonable timelines ultimately comes down to striking a balance between realism and ambition and producing both attainable and significant outcomes.

This plan will ensure everything gets done without being chaotic or out of control.

A strategy like this is essential for efficient time management since it ensures everything gets done without feeling chaotic or out of control.

When something unexpected happens, which it always does, you may adjust the strategy without losing sight of your ultimate objective or becoming scared. After teaching adults how to manage their time for years, if there's one thing I've learned, it's that managing your life is a lot like doing laundry. You need a schedule that allows you to maintain organization and cleanliness while allowing yourself some leeway for spontaneity.

Plan your schedule wisely and ensure it contains both work and leisure time to avoid much stress.

It's very simple for someone busy to become mired in the daily grind. There is always something to do—at work, at home, with the family—and not enough time. Stress can result from this, negatively affecting the body and mind. Here are some pointers on how to plan your time such that it contains both work and lots of downtime to reduce stress and simplify your life:

Determine which of your top priorities are. If you're unsure what they are, give them some serious thought until you do!

● Write down all the chores or things that need to be done. Next, rank each item on the list in order of importance (for example, if one task has an urgent deadline while another does not). When two jobs are equally urgent, decide which one would benefit from finishing first. For instance, "Fixing the leaky pipe" might be more important than "Clearing out my inbox."

Calculate the amount of time you now dedicate to your main objectives.

Finding out how much time you spend on your main objectives is the first step in time management. Though challenging, this isn't as difficult as it seems. This could be an excellent time to pause and determine your goals if you aren't sure what they are. Write down everything significant to you or propels your life forward to do this (for example, family relationships or financial security). Create a list of every job required to accomplish these objectives now. As an illustration:

Acquiring Knowledge of French

Composing a book

● Purchasing a home

Determine the most critical tasks and devise strategies for completing them.

● Select the most critical tasks and devise strategies to complete them.

● Selecting what to work on first when you have a lot on your plate might be challenging. If you're lucky, one task or objective will be the most significant for the day and should be prioritized over everything else. However, this isn't always the case.

● One workaround for this issue is to prioritize your daily duties so that you begin each day by accomplishing something worthwhile (or close to it). So, when considering how to make the most of your workday, keep an eye out for fresh opportunities! These could include locating underutilized resources within a company or industry and speaking engagements for staff members like you who represent different departments within their company, like marketing teams!

Make time in your schedule for activities that make you feel good about yourself and fulfilled but not so much that they detract from your main objectives.

We all have ambitions, perhaps even lofty ones, but trying to do everything at once can lead to several distractions from our true purpose in life. If you want to succeed at something, make sure it's your priority and then plan self-care time daily or weekly (or whatever works best). Your general health will improve with more work, so play your balance!

Timestamp Management ForHardwareren And Parents

Being a busy parent and juggling work, family, and personal obligations can be difficult. Effective time management skills are essential to remaining organized, preserving your well-being wellbeing, and making sure your family prospers in the face of many demands on your time. In this detailed, scientific, and practical guide, we'll look at proven time management tactics for busy parents and give real-world examples and advice to help you strike a balance between your profession, family, and personal life.

The Time Management Science for Busy Parents

Research on time management and psychology has shown that effective time management is critical for overall productivity, stress reduction, and wellbeing. Studies show that parents who effectively manage their time experience lower stress levels, higher happiness in both their personal and professional lives, and more free time for hobbies and self-care.

Set priorities and goals.

Set realistic goals and priorities for the beginning of your personal and professional lives. Make a list of your top priorities and schedule your time accordingly. Setting priorities for your tasks will help you focus on what matters most and keep from feeling overworked.

Real-Life Example: A married professional lady values meeting deadlines, getting regular exercise, and having quality time with her kids. She sets goals for each priority, including seeing her kids for at least an hour daily, finishing her work on time, and working out thrice weekly.

Practical Tip: Use a planner or digital calendar to list your objectives and monitor your progress. Regularly review and revise your objectives.

Schedule and Arrangement

Planning and scheduling are essential time management skills for working parents. Commitments to your family, your job, your time, and any other duties you have to juggle.

A busy father plans his week's events, including business meetings, his kids' soccer lessons, supper preparation, and alone time for reading or working out. He talks with his wife about this agenda to keep everyone informed and plan their family's activities.

Use a family scheduling program or a shared digital calendar to reduce arguments and keep everyone informed. There should be sharing and delegation of responsibilities.

Sharing responsibilities and assigning jobs to your spouse, family, and other support systems is essential if you're a busy parent. By doing this, you'll be able to reduce your workload and make more time for hobbies and other essential tasks.

A working mother assigned her husband and kids age-appropriate household chores, including vacuuming, dishwashing, and laundry. She also arranges for other parents to carpool so that the stress of getting kids to extracurricular activities can be shared.

Practical Tip: To ensure everyone is on the same page, discuss task delegation with your spouse and kids and create a chore chart or shared task list.

Don't Get Sidetracked and Establish Limits

Effective time management requires establishing boundaries between work and personal life. Set aside specific times for business, and don't take calls or check emails while spending time with family or friends. Minimize interruptions during concentrated work or family time, such as social media use and excessive multitasking.

Real-World Example: After 6 p.m., a working parent sets a limit by refusing to check work emails. Or during the weekends. They also establish a distraction-free work environment by setting up a home workstation and turning off social media notifications during work hours.

Use app timers or internet blockers to lessen the number of distractions you encounter when working or spending time with your family. Share your boundaries with friends, family, and coworkers to minimize disruptions.

Accept flexibility and adaptability.

Circumstances and changes. Recognize adaptability and flexibility by adjusting your priorities and timetable as needed, and be willing to rearrange your responsibilities in order of importance.

The parent-child work meeting is rescheduled to accommodate their child's school function. They make accommodations by assigning a coworker to lead the meeting, rescheduling it, or getting a family member to go to the school function in their place.

Practical Tip: Regularly check and update your calendar to account for unforeseen occurrences and shifting priorities.

Make personal time a priority and take care of yourself.

Overly busy parents often neglect their wellbeing and hobbies, which can result in burnout and lower output. Prioritize your wellbeing by scheduling regular time for socialization, hobbies, exercise, and relaxation.

Real-Life Example: A busy mother dedicates thirty minutes daily to reading, meditation, or brisk walks to decompress and relieve stress. They schedule regular date evenings with their partner and get together with pals.

Practical Tip: Schedule personal time and self-care as vital appointments. Encourage your spouse and kids to do the same to create a happy, healthy family atmosphere.

Utilize Time-Saving Techniques and Resources

Make the most of time-saving tips and resources to streamline your everyday schedule, such as meal planning, online grocery shopping, and productivity apps to help you keep organized.

Real-World Example: A busy mom orders groceries online and prepares their meals for the week to avoid making time-consuming trips to the market. They organize their to-do list and keep track of their daily tasks using productivity tools.

Practical Tip: Look into various time-saving devices and methods, then incorporate the ones that suit your family and way of life the best into your daily schedule.

It can be difficult to balance job, family, and personal commitments when you're a busy parent. Still, you can maintain your wellbeing and attain peace by learning efficient time management skills. You may simplify your daily schedule and free up more time for the things that matter by setting priorities, making a plan, scheduling, assigning tasks, setting limits, accepting flexibility, taking care of yourself, and using time-saving technologies. With this comprehensive, scientific, and useful handbook, busy parents can easily manage job and family life demands while cultivating their interests and wellbeing.

An individual can gain from effective time management. It eases stress and improves overall wellbeing. The importance of effective time management increases when you are taking care of an elderly parent.

After all, each day has only 24 hours. But they are probably already full of work, caring for your family, and juggling everything else; now, you're adding elderly loved ones' caregiving duties. How, then, can you maintain your composure and be the person who matters to everyone?

Arrange and Obtain a High Perspective

Many books on business recommend creating a weekly plan. Caregivers can benefit from this similar idea.

On Sunday evening, take ten minutes to work with your calendar. Look over the upcoming week to see what's planned. Can you put any addresses or phone numbers into your calendar now so you won't have to search for them later? This week, where could you need a little extra support? Is there anything you can reschedule at this time?

If you do this simple action every week, it will make every Monday morning more bearable.

Make a list of things to do.

It's easy to lose important minutes of the day when you're not organized. Creating a list will assist you in staying focused. Give your daily to-do list some thought and rank them in order of importance.

Start by noting the things that are hard to plan for, such as your parents' doctor appointments. Organizing your calendar with scheduled appointments makes it simpler to fit other tasks around them.

Which chores or errands are you dreading the most? To give the rest of your week a boost, finish those first. Whenever I dread a chore, I usually do this, and it feels so good to finish it and mark it off my list.

Do not forget to save at least one block of time as a "catch-all." During this period, finish up any unfinished business and make calls. Start there. I find that scheduling this chunk of time throughout the week works best. If another day works better for you, you can easily move that time to next week.

Recruit or employ help.

Giving up even the most basic obligations can be incredibly relieving, and those tiny things can occasionally build up to a lot. What regular obligations do your children, spouse, or siblings have? Maybe someone can take your loved one to their weekly hair appointment or pick up their monthly medicines. Your parent's neighbours might want to help, so be ready with ideas for possible activities.

Similarly, accept a kind offer of help from a valued friend and assign them a task from your list. We decline requests occasionally to avoid disturbing others, but your friends wouldn't extend an offer if they weren't earnest in their want to assist. Accept their offer from them.

Employed assistance can also lessen your responsibilities. Consider getting a cleaner to do the deep cleaning twice a month while you do the occasional tidying. Hire a neighbourhood child to mow the lawn three times a week or walk the dog. Consider using services like Snap Kitchen for meal preparation or grocery delivery. Take advantage of the fact that the internet has made it easier to find trustworthy people or businesses to assist you with these responsibilities.

Give up trying to be flawless.

You must occasionally give yourself a break because you have so much on your plate. Nobody expects you to cook meals of Martha Stewart calibre when you have a family and a job and care for one or more other people.

Remember to Take Care of Yourself

In keeping with that, caregivers often prioritize others before themselves, but only you can ensure that you have enough fuel in your tank.

Make time each week for "me time"—a 30-minute massage that relieves tension, a coffee date with a close friend, or simply some alone time with a good book. To ensure you don't forget about it, mark it as your mental health break on your calendar.

Get Ready to Take It On

Accidents happen, and when they throw off your carefully plotted routine, it's normal to feel anxious. But since these things do happen, learn to prepare for them in advance to make the experience less unpleasant when it does. Acknowledge them, inhale deeply, and face them.

Page Nine

Time Management for Authors and Writers: To ensure they are working on their projects steadily, writers should establish a regular writing plan and daily word count targets.

Time Management and Continuous Feedback Loops: To find bottlenecks or inefficiencies in your time management procedures, set up feedback loops with coworkers, mentors, or superiors.

Time Management for Healthcare Administrators: By implementing effective scheduling systems, cutting down on administrative burdens, and better allocating resources, healthcare administrators may maximize patient care.

Time management and focused reading: Increase the effectiveness of your reading by employing strategies such as selective or speed reading, where you concentrate on the most important information and skip over less important passages.

Online business owners should prioritize tasks that generate the highest revenue and use analytics and data-driven insights to improve their marketing efforts. This is known as time management for online entrepreneurs.

Time Management for Multilingual Learning: Make a planned study schedule and use resources and applications for language learning if you're learning multiple languages simultaneously.

Time Management for Research and Development: To effectively spur innovation, researchers and innovators might set aside particular times for experimenting, brainstorming, and problem-solving.

Time Management for Musicians: Musicians can maximize

their practice regimens by utilizing time management strategies such as the "deliberate practice" paradigm, which concentrates on targeted skill development.

Time management for athletes: To ensure they reach their full performance potential, athletes can utilize time management to organize their diet, training, and recovery regimens.

Time Management for Philanthropists: Those who practice philanthropy should set aside time for thoughtful grant selection, assessing the effect of donations, and interacting with nonprofits.

Time management skills and emotional intelligence are closely related.

Setting aside time for environmental sustainability-promoting activities, such as recycling, conservation, and volunteer work on green projects, is a crucial aspect of time management.

Time management and parenting: By learning to manage their time effectively, parents may ensure they spend quality time with their partners and children while juggling work, family, and personal obligations.

Time Management for Historians: To effectively arrange and examine historical material and sources, historians can use digital archival technologies and research management software.

Time Management for Supply Chain Managers: Supply chain experts may streamline operations by putting in place just-in-time inventory systems and utilizing data analytics to shorten lead times.

Effective time management techniques can help lawyers and other legal professionals handle cases, prepare documents, and communicate with clients more quickly.

Time Management for Regular Travelers: Passengers can utilize travel applications to organize their itineraries, plan their journeys in great detail, and utilize their downtime for business or leisure while travelling.

Time Management and Space Organization: Set up your digital and physical work areas efficiently to reduce your time looking for information or supplies.

Time management and Social Media Engagement: Plan dedicated time slots for content production, interaction, and analytics analysis if you utilize social media for personal or professional branding.

Time Management and Mindful Decision-Making: Develop mindfulness techniques to help you choose thoughtfully and deliberately rather than impulsively in response to outside demands or distractions.

Time Management for Emergency Responders: Emergency responders can effectively manage personnel and resources by utilizing incident command systems and response plans.

Time Management for Competitive Examinations: To ace your examinations, develop study plans, test-taking tactics, and time management strategies before competitive exams.

Time Management for Event Managers: From venue selection to post-event review, event managers can simplify event logistics using collaboration tools and event planning software.

Time Management for Personal Development Retreats: Set aside time regularly for self-reflection, goal-setting, and skill-building exercises that are part of personal development retreats.

Time Management for Risk Assessment: Set aside time for risk analysis and backup plans to ensure you're ready for unforeseen difficulties and emergencies.

www.ingramcontent.com/pod-product-compliance
Lightning Source LLC
Chambersburg PA
CBHW052142110526
44591CB00012B/1824